TRUCULENT
Writings 'n' Poetry

TRUCULENT
Writings 'n' Poetry

By
Michael J. Stuckey Jr.

"Stuckey Publishing 2017"

(Disclaimer)

Warning — Disclaimer

Born in the summer of 1977, Michael said, "I have Worked 38 Jobs & Hated almost all of them. At one time or another I've Owned, Ran & Sold 3 Company's. I Tried Every Type of Drink & Drug. I have had the opportunity to travel and see many parts of the world, including 4 Island's. I Have 1 Son, while Infatuated with his mother we got Married. the Ceremony was held by a High Priestess, in the Eye's of the Goddess of Love & the Goddess of Night.

My life has been painfully fortunate. I've Done Every to do Erg, Morally Wrong or Right. Each Bad Judgment, Sexual Fantasy, Impulse's & Desire I Have Fulfilled. I Flat Lined 4 times, Evan Fell In-Love once, which i found to be the one and only thing that scared the hell out of me! Unfortunately all the Lessons In-which I've Learned, have been nothing short of the Hard Way.

Poetry I have written reflects: Romance, Love, Trivial, Dark, Deceptive, Heartbreak, & Sadistic Writing's.

Index

CONTENTS

4 *Atheist Scripture's*   77

Short Note:

Begin With: Dolor
Through: Adjy
By the end of: Truculent
Understanding you will have.

Infliction of Pain through torture
Received & Given Graciously..
Love & Hatred wheeled methodically.
Your Intellectual Suffering,
Emotional Conflict-ion,
My Welcoming.

The Old One's

Siren

Birthed on Island of Arouse,
Enticed by her song,
Obedience she will demand,
Compelled to please her.
Your will forgone,
Your clothes like your hide,
Pealed off.
Unable to scream,
To release the pain.
A body suit to be worn,
Enticing her next Victim.

Rightful Place

Branches & Twigs,
Cat Tails lashed together,
Black Label pored over,
Silver Coin on each Eye,
Torched adrift.
Thy Ascension,
To sit along side the Gods.

Father Of

Moments of despair,
People catch a glimpse of me.
While payback & vengeance pursued,
People use me.
While Honor & Pride are held,
People accept all of me.

Many Names I've been called.
Daemon, Satan, Devil, God,
Thy Name, Angellous.

I nurture Man & Woman's
Thoughts, Desire, Ambitions & Actions.
When you need me, I will be there.

People say, "sell your Soul"
Before your Birth,
During your Life & after your Death
Soul Not Yours To Sell...

As Father,
My Children are you.
Take comfort,
I Will Not Judge!!!!

Daemon Within

When you're unsure or insecure,
We are there to further encourage.
When at the end of your rope,
Can't take anymore,
You call on us, to turn from sorrow.
In the hatred we thrive.
When you lash out,
In your torment, Intrigue We have,
Ruining all that you are.

Finally lost everything you have,
Torn apart & measurable,
Begging for Death,
We take pleasure & feel alive.
Until then we'll bide our time,
Waiting for you,
To come within 'n' hide.

To Have

Elbow to Wrist slit,
Submerged in Sink.
Thy blood I offer as a fresh drink,
Goddess Helcet significant I am,
Never been Glifted, nor over drawn,
To drink of her, Be Thy Honor....

Deduction

Morbid inhibitions,
Discreet insurrection,
Yesterday's forgotten,
In today's razor.
Fire in her Eyes,
Kong-e sounded,
Four Goddesses called down,
Notions abiding,
Thirst Quenched.

Eternal

Widowed Witches Night,
Along Maple Rivers Edge.
Acting illusions,
Howling & frolicking.
Oracles by Moon's light,
Bewitching in site.
Wheeling blessing magics,
Before morning's light.

Touch of the Gods

Day's end in a Veil of Night,
Moon's glow protruding Vivacious Clouds,
Serenity of silence,
Promise of a gleaming Sun Rise.
Purity of Life,
A Graceful Awakening.

Home coming

Baled Show saw in a dream,
Glory of the coming,
False Religion,
Purity of truth,
Birth into innocence.

What was taught, Learned.
Death welcomes, An Unbelievable Kiss,
to experience an Amazing Kingdom,
Better than all the rest.

Once Knew

Eave of Birth,
Lasticity of once knew,
Events cast Crystal Waters,
Laying in Shadows,
Soul not of my own,
From the other side,
Submerged,
In a Century not of My Own.

Stone Line

Riddle Forsaken,
Touched when conceived,
Gates of Sanctuary,
Wooden Stone,
The Hornet One,
Crooked Line,
Bringer of Fate,
Profound Decadence,
A Fossil's Story.

Dwindling

Art of form,
Glimmer of light,
Now leaving my sight.
Empty words spoken,
Incantation of changes,
Moments apart.
Experience may answer,
Leaves a complex riddle.

Dark 'n' Sadistic Writings

Warning: Graphic

Fluttering Butterfly

From the back,
Softly with the tip of my Tongue,
Circling around,
Gradually & Gracefully,
Up Across the Perineum.

From the Bottom up to the top,
Delicately licking,
An Ice Cream Cone,

Continuing with the tip of my Tongue.
Rapidly flicking the Clitoris,
Pinky in Anal vibrating,
Pointer in Vagina swaying,
From side, to the top, to the side,
Thrusting in & out,
While continually & rapidly,
Flicking the Clitoris with my Tongue.

Legs Buckle and
Thighs begin fluttering,
With left hand & a sharp Athame,
Cut Across Her Lips,
Endorphins in Blood, Orgasm,
Ecstasy.

Decadence

Maybe it was the way You Looked at Me.
Maybe it was All the Drugs.
You consumed all of me,
Left an empty shell behind.
Maybe it was the Liquor,
Maybe it was the Hope,
To fill the emptiness in me.
Decadence of Payback,
All that Remains.

Between

The darkness that is of me,
The light that you've
Brought into my life.
Tearing me from the seams,
For what I've done,
Who I become,
Who I want to be,
You're Treachery unto me.

Echoes

Like Foot steps,
Echo down a hallowed hallway,
Killer walks, one House to another.
With the determination
'N' focus as if possessed.

As if his own, enters the House.
A young 20-something couple,
Lingering on their couch.
Knocks the Man out,
Binds Ankles to Wrist behind His Back,
Waits until awakes.

Tortures, Molests, Rapes,
Mutilating the young Man's Wife,
While He Watches.

Killer walks over, Laughingly
Cuts His Throat,
Gasps Last Breath,
Choking; Blood Bubbles,
Waiting to see, Soul leave His Eyes
Disgruntle & Unfulfilled,
Like Foot Steps,
Echo down a hallowed Hallway,
On to the Next.

Next House

From one Town, another,
House to House,

Raping & Plundering,
Trying to fulfill his Unsatisfied calling.

A Gothic 17 Yr old,
He sees the Scars on Her Body,
He sees the Pain in Her Eyes,
Knowing what she's been longing for.

Window he comes through,
Ties her up & hangs her on the wall,
Teaching Her what Cutting truly means,
How Cutting Truly Feels.

She begs him to continue,
To cut; not so shallow,
For the Release of Pain to be true,
To Teach Her,
What she only wished she knew.

As Foot Steps,
Echo down a Hallowed Hall,
All the while longing for the End to come,
First Victim left Alive.

Neurotic Hanging

Wrist bound,
5/8 nylon rope,
Up 'n' around her long thin neck.

5 ft. off ground,
Swinging n' Frolicking,
Bouncing around.
Tightening n' Binding,
Restricting her air.
Lights growing dim,
Now passing out,

Released to the Ground.

Reawakened to be pulled up again,
Gasping for Air,
Forced into Positions,
His Neurotic Pleasures.

Tightening n' Binding,
Restricting her air.
Only to be released,
To Start all over again.

Asked In

Glass of Wine,
Sweet Romantic nothings,
Whispered in Time.
Promise of Our Pleasures.
Bound with Curtain Tie.
Blood Letting with a Dull Athame.

Begged & Pleaded to Stop,
In the Skillet of Her Thigh,
Steak & Wine,
Sweet Romantic nothings,
Whispered in Time.

Cauterize Wounds,
Repeatedly Raped,
6 Days Infliction,
Back Yard she lay, 6 Feet under,
Insanity with a day of Air.

Center Peace

A Little Gravel,
Some Twigs,
Sprouts of Grass,
A pin through the Heart,
Spread Wings,
Perched in a Pose,
Encased in Glass,
Sheltered & Scorn,
With all Its Beauty,

Tormented Butterfly,
On my mantle.

Taken

Tears soak,
A sorrowed Heart.
My light,
To brighten your darkest door.

Repeatedly beaten n' bound,
With thousands of shallow cuts,
Hung by Her Ankles,
Left to Die,
Sister Mary Anne Catherine's,
Innocents; Violently Taken.

Only Pendants',
3 Hail Marries & 1 Grace.

Butterfly

Soft and gentle,
Breathe taking-Ly pretty.
Mystical tease,
Delicate of touch,
Not that of fragile,
Only that of gentle braes.
Seemingly of grace.
A mirror she is,
To stages of her life.
My Butterfly,
An Essence of Infinity.

Chorus

Give you what you want,
Give you what you need,
You gave me nothing,
You take from me everything,
Give you time to be,
Tell you just how to please me,
You exist to fulfill,
My Sadistic Tendency.
You are,
Cause I allow you to be.

Label

At the tip of the Knife,
I can only win,
To Cleanse,
To no longer dwindle in.
Adrenalin partakes a Fool's Rush,
Labeled this & Labeled that,
Government Semantics.

Bound Mystically,
Drugged up & released,
Locked emptiness within,

Everything will be alright.

Lines

Innocence tossed away,
Rhythm of life blinded,
Changing a Tormented Soul,
Either from a Jar,
Pinky Ring,
A dash on the Hand,
On a Mirror,
Or off Her Body.
To ease into calm,
To feel something,
Salutations,
To those who have gone.

Invited

Young 'n' stupid,
Pure of vigilance,
Tempted by eternal night.
Kiss of darkness,
Demented pleasures in sight.
With arm's open,
Took from thee,
Life shown to you.
Never to see Light of Day.

Caught

Drama of versatility,
Lines of antiquity
Colors of anti-quality,
Torn between tranquility & divinity,
Temptations of lust,
Free of regret,
Seduction of masochism,
Sins of trust.
Divination,
Only in love & death.

Can Not Dream

I lay in my bed wide awake,
For if I sleep,
Dreams of horrors
Rush all through my head,
Too many voices,
Too many screams,
I can not sleep,
I lay here awake,
Awaiting the night's Dream.

Unsolved

Nylon hooded ski mask,
Surgical gloves,
Turtleneck & jeans,
A single twin edge Blade,
Leaving no trace.

Timing and held content,
Pleasure in act of Mutilation,
Satisfaction in their Suffering.

Jane or John Doe.
Cup of their blood,
Before the last drop.
Back of the neck,
Enochian Glyph engraved.
Enslaving their Soul,
Bound to me,
As a Servant to a Master.

One's Life

From Streets of Camelot,
Rivers of Babylon,
To Clubs of Cities.

Some dream of our reality,
Some are fake.
We're not of Saints,
Nor of Demon.

Rituals, Blood Lettings,
Massacre, Slaughter,
& Treacherous acts.
Drink of Body,
Occasionally from Goblet Glass.

With solis; Black Veil we abide,
Bound to gather by Honor,
Living through Death, Confined.

Vulparia

Tribulations,
Fixations,
Erotic Asphyxiation.
Non delinquent,
Of painful pleasures.
Neurotic tendency,
In seduction of desire.

No contemplations,
Paralyzed by
Forgone Actions.

Gilded

Moon's energy I thrive.
Linger in the day,
Stalking Thy Pray,
Victim they'll be,
Transgression is mine.

Infliction of desire,
Blood & Chocolate,
Meat & Wine,
Death & Anguish,
That which I bring.

Thy craving of
Pleasure in all that
Walks around....

Broken Doll

19; Bruised & Cut,
Strong toned legs,
Tight perfect gluteus,
Skin; bronzed,
Can't keep hands off.

Slight lines, of a toned stomach.
Shape of pear, firm perky breast,
Body electrocuted daily.
Diamonds draped around a bound neck.
Long, matted, deep satin black hair.

Fresh; Sweat,
Taste of citrus & strawberry.
Stolen virginity,

Vigorously & repeatedly, Violated.

Start to finish protected as she learns,
Video taped, Hundreds of posed pictures,
With Her last breath,
She asked am I Pretty?

Clear Plastic wrapped,
To let you see.
Her bright iridescent,
Green Soulless Eye's.
This Forsaken Beauty,
Stayed Willingly.

Forsaken Beauty

Chained to a Stone Wall

Tells Me;
I'm a Disgrace,
I'm a Slob & I'm Ugly,
That I am Nothing.

Tells Me;
When I can Eat & Drink,
When I can go to the Bathroom,
What Clothes I can Wear.

Chained to a Stone Wall

Tells Me;
Through Pain,
I Will Learn to Obey.
Through Depravity,

I will Learn to be Grateful.
In Time I Will Become,
Respectful; Disciplined & Loyal.
I will be Worthy to be called a Woman,
That I Will Be Pretty.

Chained to a Stone Wall
Forward I Look,
Subservient & Willing,
Occasionally Cuts, Electrocutes &
Or Chokes Me,

As He Has His Way With Me.
Dresses Me & Teaches Me.

All While I Hope,
I Will No Longer be, a Broken Doll.
I Will Become His Wife,
Unchained from this Stone Wall.
Will He Keep Me?

Taught

Tribulations of belief,
Contemplating Life,
Through failed suicide,
Pleasures of heart,
Pleasures of skin,
Painful hear in,
Insurrection beaten in,
Existential Suffering.

Anticipation

These chains that Bind,
Can not confine,
Drift off to Exotic Worlds,
Places been,
Photographs seen,
Images of Islands to be.

As I Day Dream they come.
Like a Raging Doll,
They Play with Me.
When I'm Quiet ... they're rough,
When I Scream ... they're Satisfied,
Lucky I Am,
When the End Comes.

Conscious

Cool Clear Blue Waters,
Rotting Hull of Steel,
Drops of blood Thy road home.
Truly experience Truculent,
Episodes called a grateful life.

Hindering Demons,
Only Enhance a Succulent Soul,
Of Fleeting Suicides.
Distortion of Society.

Sealed

Captured,
Diminished of Spirit,
Within you,
Extinguished Fire.

Picture & Locket of Hair,
Together by Leather Twine,
Wax Sealed blessed Jar.
Your soul as my Servant,
Eternally Intertwined.

Consenting

From the Door, Slammed to the Floor,
Behind Back Wrist Bound & Ankles Strapped,
Mouth Gagged; Tearing Eyes flowing down,
Sultrily Groping, Feeling & Tasting.

Hang by the Wrist,
Around Torso Separately Binding each Breast,
Nipple Clips, Stainless Steel Blade,
Body Cries Tears of Blood.

A few Smacks,
Legs Pulled up Knees Spread Apart,
Violated slow to rough,
UN-hung & still tied up.
Multiple positions repeatedly,
Haven't had enough.

Hog Tied in the corner,
Sponge and bowl of water,
Getting washed up,
Notice Camera above the Door.

She Asked:
Am I First BDSM? Or Placed in a collection?
When,
When Can We Do It Again???

Follow Through

Things told you,
Past events & current motions,
No Regrets,
Only you're Sorrow.
Place here is no longer.
Awaiting Death's Lackey
Done by hands,
Fixation will be fulfilled.

Not Unlike

Inflamed all the time,
Hurts when aggravated,
Annoying no matter what,
Can't get away from it,
Nor hide from,
This life not unlike an
Abrasion.

A Lead

Carnage of a Massacre.
Demolition of the Rapture.
Serenity of Conception.
As I read your words,
Your Poem comes to end,
Words I'm falling form,
Evaporating in warm mist,
Leaving me in Angst for your next.

Vengeance

Financial loss,
Freedom taken & Violated,
Punk in Cell Block B.
Family Tortured passed away,
Remainder of his life foretold.

When released,
Nothing He will have,
Mutilated & Still Breathing,
Cramped box, 'n' Buried Alive,
The way of your Demise,
Only chance of Vindication.

Chemical

Cut you deep,
Cut you shallow,
Rubbed in Lye,
Watched as surface boiled,
Liquidizing underneath,
Watched as it oozed out,
From under the Skin.

Almost out of Reach,
Bottle of Vinegar to neutralize,
Switched with Water.

In Your Scream,
Excruciating,
Stinging; Painful Horrific Burn,
This is Just the Beginning.

Spun Web

Nights light blinded sight,
Chains that bind,
Bleeding heart of mine,
Cocoon wrapped tight,
Truculent experiences bound with you,
Your Veil cast,
Dangling on Tarantula's Web.

Being with You,
Autoerotic Asphyxiation.

Bleeding Thorns

Still in the day,
Moments of glee,
Lynched,
With memories of sorrow.

Poems of bleeding colors,
High bread Roses,
Day of vine intertwine,
Thorns drawing blood,
With each memory of glee.

Creeper

Arrived as your friend,
Took you in the den,
On the balcony I left your
Mother with a smiling grin.

Over the railing, a single molt scotch,
Spilled from the glass.
Laundry; spin cycle starts,
Your Aunt finishes off.

Dinner time; Sister hands on,
Drink my wine,
Can't help but shine.

As your Father asked, What's your intentions?

Laughing I answered, Creeping!
Left your Daughter bruised & sore,
Your Wife's bleeding again,
Your Sister is a pregnant bore,
& your youngest Daughter is under the table,
Good little Whore.

7 long hours,
Thy Intentions are no more.

Ritual

Black beauty to rise,
Yellow jacket to get going,
2 eight balls for work,

The ride home; 1 eight ball,
2 Roxy with a Beer,
Take a shower, smoke an L.
Got the munchies, cruising now.
Returning phone calls,
Stepping out to meet the crew.
Dance club another eight ball,
2 triple stack green diamonds,
Orange juice a must.

Serviced in bathroom,
Multiple numbers in hand,
Taking another home.

Wake up,
Tell her to get out,
Black beauty; we start again.

Cutting

The sweet sensation,
Sliding across my thigh,
The stinging the burning,
Releasing my inhibitions.
A little deeper a little longer,
Dragging smoothly across my chest.

Now I feel it.
The truth it's pure,
The warmth of my blood,
The serenity of the blade,
Intoxicating.

Forearm now open.
The comfort, the pain,
The neurotic tease of metal separating the skin.
My release from this mortal coil,
A knife's edge, so seductive.

Like Blood

You're a Liar.
I Fucking Hate You.
You Act Like a Succubus,
I can't fucking Stand You.
You Take Every Thing from Me,
Give Nothing In Return,
You're a Waste of My Time,
Stay the Fuck Away From Me.
You're Playing Games Again,
You Fucking Psycho.
Like Blood is to Life,
You're My Everything,
FUCK,
All I Want is you.

Death

A Hold on Me

Thou time heals all wounds,
Memories of You still Haunt Me,
Emotions for You still Hold Me,
Tears continue to fall,
Love we had can not be Erased,
Permanently Damaged,
Thou time Heals all wounds,
Still I wait to be released.

Contract

3:27 Picked Lock,
Buckshot Blast,
To his Wife's Chest,

Forced to write a Note:
This Cheating Whore,
Caused this, & Singed.

Knocked-out & Sat-up,
Shotgun Placed in His Hands,
Propped from the Floor,
Barrel in his mouth,
As He Awakes,
Trigger is pulled.

A Murder; Suicide,
38 Grand &,
A Train Ticket Home.

Heretic

Every miss-dead,
A turn of the crank,
For each done to others,
A lashing received,
Mind turns 'n' wonders off,
Laughing outside.

To confess Your Sins,
Plead Allegiance to their Religion,
A Quickening it will be,

However,
Of Thy Heresy?
Continued Dismemberment,
It will be.
Scattered to the Furthest Corners,
For the World to See,
A Martyr You will now be.

Passed On

Scared,
I Hide from The Man I am.
What I've Endured,
An Enemy shouldn't.

Notion of a Body,
But none to find or feel.
No Loved Ones,
Nor Forgotten One's Waiting.
Pain, Sorrow & Misery,
Non Existent.
No thought of feeling,
Serenity; an Empty Void,
Taste of Divination.

Making Rite

Sternum to hip delicately slit,
Skin deep,
Entrails exposed.
Slowly draw out innards.
Tied to a back stand,
Kerosene & a match,
Watching him gasping to Scream,
Fire-y air burning his lungs.
Pride taken in His Death.

Tribulations

Insurrections of fate,
Validation gone wrong,
Vulgar complexity,
Inside like a Numbing Epidural,
Followed through,
Accomplished Convictions.

Corinarius Orellanus

20 Mg. per Kg. Body weight
Mixed with wine.
Yet eager to gulp,
Must sip; Indulging in an orgasm of taste.

20 minutes till blood stream,
Anticipation sets in.
White blood cells multiplying,
Adrenalin kicking in,
Kidney's killing,
Can't sit still, loosen it,
Climbing out of my skull.

White cells double – triple.
Rapidly multiplying.
Getting hard to breathe now,
Renal failure,
Energy running out,

Anxiety setting in,
To late for the doc,
Sluggish & cold,
Painfully slow,
Two hours or less; Cardiac Arrest.

Another Failure

5/8th. rope 30 feet long,
Parked against a tall Tree,
Over a branch tied at the base,
Loop with 11 rings & pulled through,
Slid tight around the neck,
Step off the Truck,
Dangling; losing consciousness,
Rope gave, feet on the ground,
How Disappointing.

A Waist

Glass rose,
Another rock,
Deep pull; a long inhale,
Hoping to fill the hole,
Hoping heart will implode.

Out of rock n' glass cracking,
No more money, fig-get-in.
Jones-in, heart still beating,
2 hrs 300 dollars,
Pissed off & breathing,
Getting sober again.

Known to Me

Treachery, Infliction,
Betrayal, Manipulation,
Heresy, Anarchy,
Deceit, Loyalty,
Devotion, Honor,
Dignity, Courage,
Trust & Pride.

All are of a Man.
Learned in pain,
Wheeled in Vengeance.
Controlled only,
If with no Conscious.

With fulfilled Convictions,
Virtues these will be.
In life,
A Righteous Death you will have.

One Day

Never say the right thing,
Never do the right anything.

One Day You'll come home,

Brilliantly in red,
On the Walls,
Blood Screamingly Reads.
Do You Now Approve?

As I Lie,
Dead on the floor.

What's Now?

To see what I've seen,
To do the things That which I've done.
To not feel Remorse & Guilt.
Indulge in ones Suffering & Dis-pare.
To Revel when they're truly Measurable,
Pleading for the end to be near.
Who I once was.
Now; know what is to feel?
Longing for the End,
To be near.

Of Sorts

Divulge Ones past,
Pacifist Congregation,
Sacrifice of Disciples,
Trusted in Mutilation,
Their Death for My Life,
Predication of One.

Manic

Tossing 'n' Turning Bored out of my mind.
11 o'clock
A bunch of pain killers, A few sleeping pills.
3:30 Awake. Why?
No interest or desire to get up,
To face another day.

How I love flavors of food,
Yet no longer hold a taste for it.
Explosion of taste buds as chocolate melts around.
Nauseous from cravings,
Hunger no more.
A fein for coffee, only replenishment.

Climbing out of my skin,
Have to do something, anything,
Clean out my Truck, Yard work,

Internet killing time.
Go for a ride,
2 packs of smokes,
3 finger glass; Johnny Black Label.
Bunch of pills,
Repeating; first time tears fall,
Begging; for the end of it all.

Violation of Rights

Laying on the ground, truck mangled,
Femur sticking out,
Knee turned sideways & crushed,
Foot backwards,
Off duty cop chasing, barefoot.

Now holding me still,
Trying to calm,
EMS looking to amputate,
Pleaded & begged,
Excruciating, they replied.

Morphine not working,
Resetting the femur,
Knee goes flat,
More Morphine with a
Double dose of Dilaudid,
Straightening the foot, Still awake.

Hospital; in surgery now,
Can't put me out.
Anastasia not strong enough.
Another shot, Pass out.

Recovery room awake freaking out,
Realizing; still have my leg

Mentally at ease,
Like an explosion all the drugs rush in,
Passing out, heart erratic,

Flat-line,
They're doing CPR, Screaming DNR,
Epinephrine shot, Defibrillator shock.

Stabilizing; here comes the rush,
Emotions flood, hearts breaking,
Mentally wrenched.

Torn apart 'n' mangled,
Charity-care for treatment,
17 months latter,
Still wishing they left me dead.

Contrite

Predications,
Of One's past.
Only hinder Loved Ones.
Cong-rue,
Of One's current doings.
Depict events,
Upon Love Ones.
Emotions convict us.
There is no Escape.

Screaming Souls

Pure White 'n' Unbreakable,
Rambunctious Children frolicking above.
Deep, Dark, Murky
Cold & Pain-full Death Lays Beneath.
Ice Lake; of CaTouga Bay.

My Hope

My world will never be
Anything I hoped for.
I'm afraid what you'll find,
In me there's nothing.
All I want
Is For this life to End.

Brethren

Profits are Nun,
Witch's, Warlock's as one,
Goddesses of Gods,
Daemons of Fallen Saints,
Long for Helcet to Kiss,
Last of a Dying deepest Fear,
To Join My Family,
To be told,
Welcomed Home.

Atheist
Scriptures

Final breath

How pleasing,
My sins are unto you.
Forgive me not, cleanse me not.
Thy soul finds it pleasing.
In my heart; let Thy rest come,
May I find my sleep.

They self god

I Thyself above all things,
Believe that I am of god.
I long for release of Thy soul.
Since I cannot receive Sacrament,
My heart at least free of Discretion.
Since I belong alongside the Gods,
I embrace myself & entirely to Thy self.

Merciful

I give thanks with all of my Soul
For any & all mercies, graces,
I have earned Thyself,
For never prostrating at any man's feet,
I offer nothing more than myself in life or death!
With my whole Soul,
All my treason against you,
All the abominations and sins of my past life.
I renew promises I made,
And from this moment,
I dedicate myself to the service of Thy self.
Time come to past,
I may not detest sin or death itself,
To smite all such occasions and companies
Which I have regret & brought me to it.
This I resolve to do by Thy own divine grace.

Sick

I am eternally of a God,
Thy essence everlasting,
Hear me, thy servant,
We ask the aid of thee,
Brothers & Sisters,
Restore this body's health,
For which I give thanks.

Who Suffer

May it rain?
For those who suffer,
For no one to see the tears,
Of those who cry this night,
Give them repose of their burdens.
Let there be moments,
Where they experience peace,
When others cannot.
May I find understanding?

Healing

Your invite,
To all who are burdened?
Ask for healing unto me.
My soul & compassion for others.
My heart & courage for all.
My mind & your wisdom,
That I may always proclaim.
Teach me to reach within,
To end my need,
Help me to lead others by my example.
Touch gently this life,
Now and forever.

Spirit

May Thy Spirit be bold today,
Fill me with gifts of
Wisdom, discernment, knowledge,
Understanding, compassion,
Love, and to awe in no man's presence.
In all that I think, say, and do,
Let it be in accordance
With Thy perfect will.

Our Father

Thy self,
Be Thy name,
Thy kingdom will rise,
As Thy will be done.
Smite our trespassers,
Who trespass against us,
Lead us into Temptation,
Deliver us the ability of Evil.

To See

Please help me understand
The world I can not change . . .
To see the way . . .
To see a better world . . .
Not that of Thy own....

Of thy self

I asked for strength to achieve,
I asked that I might do great things,
I was not made weak.

I asked for riches,
I was given poverty.
I asked for the praise of men.
I was given weakness.

May I learn to be humble...
May I learn to be wise...
May I learn the need for the God's...
I asked to enjoy Life.
I was given Truculent experiences of all things...

I got nothing I asked for & nothing I had hoped for,
Despite the Gods; my desires fulfilled.
I am most richly blessed!

Creed

I believe in Thy self,
Who was conceived by spirit,
Born of the suffered,
I died, descended into hell,
Ascended into heaven and cast back down to man,
From thence, judged by the living and the dead.
I believe in the Spirit of Thy self,
The Old Religion and life everlasting.

Of strength

Allow me the strength,
Defend Thy self in battle,
Defense against the wickedness,
And snares of man.
Allow me the Courage,
fulfill Thy convictions,
And smite all the other spirits,
Who prowl about the world,
Seeking the ruin of Thy soul.

Rightful seat

May Thy Soul be of divination?
Body be of tranquility,
Blood of the weak to quench Thy thirst,
Sins for their death to wash me clean,
Thy wounds strengthen me,
Defend Thy self from Thy enemy,
And call me at the hour of my death,
To sit along side the Gods of the Old Religion,
That I might regain my place with them,
For all eternity.

Memorial

Remember,
That any one who attended,
To Thy protection,
Received Thy help.
Thy insurrection,
Was left unaided.
Inspired by Thy own confidence,
Unto no one before Thy self,
Before no one stand,
Before no one bow,
We of all sin,
The Word Incarnate,
Despise not our convictions,

Prayer of heretic

I am heart-full for having offended thee,
And I detest all religions,
Of greed, of obedience & control,
But most of all because,
They have offended my God; Thy self,
Who is deserving of all,
I firmly resolve with Thy grace,
Because Thy just of righteousness,
Thy will not worship:
The Father, the Son, the Holy Ghost,
Your Saints, Angels, Demands, or your God.
Vow to sin more,
And to avoid False Religions.

Grace

We give thanks to the Old Ones,
For all Thy benefits,
Who has seen world without end.
May the souls of the faithfully departed,
Rest in peace.

Trilogy of Writing's

Author: Michael J. Stuckey Jr.

Dolor: Poetry n' Writing's of Romance &
Deception (**UN-Edited)**

Stuckey's Venison Recipes:
 Wild game, Deer, recipes

Eluded Confession: Novel

Dolor; Deceived by Love: Poetry pertaining to the
deception on finds in romance.

Adjy; of treacherous, Deceptive & significant
Poetry 'n' Writing's

Truculent: of Trivial, Dark, General, Treacherous
& Sadistic Poetry 'n' Writings